CHEF'S WAY

Sage Russell

Copyright © 2012 by Conceptnine, Walnut, CA

All rights reserved. Printed in the United States of America
No part of this publication may be reproduced, stored in a retrieval system, or transmitted in any form or by any means, electronic, mechanical, photocopying, recording, scanning, or otherwise, except as permitted under section 107 or 108 of the 1976 United States Copyright Act without the prior written permission of the publisher. Requests for permission or further information should be addressed to: Permissions, Conceptnine, 340 South Lemon Ave., #4545, Walnut, CA 91789

Library of Congress Cataloguing in Publication Data

Russell, Sage.
The Chef's Way / by Sage Russell.
p. cm.
Includes index.
ISBN-13: 978-0-9800617-2-7
ISBN-10: 0-9800617-2-5
Library of Congress Control Number: 2012918785
1. Cookery. 2. Cookery – Study and Teaching. 3. Cooks – Training of. I. Russell, Sage II. Title

1.1T
10 9 8 7 6 5 4 3 2 1

THE MISSION

"A good meal shared with good people leaves the soul craving little else."

This was my premise when I left the corporate world and set off on my Food Pilgrimage mission to travel the world in search of food culture. I didn't know exactly what I wanted to bring back. I only knew that I wanted to inspire people to care more about food; learning about it, cooking it, and sharing it with people.

Through my travels - from South America to Southeast Asia, from Europe to Africa - I was constantly in awe of the little tricks and techniques that allowed cooks to wield confidence in the kitchen and serve up amazing dishes that possessed that special spark.

As I found ways to slip into restaurant kitchens, get invited to family meals and watch street food vendors work their magic, I thought *heck*, if I could share these techniques and simple tricks with you, you'd find yourself irresistibly attracted to the kitchen to try your hand at them.

This book represents those tips and tricks.

This book is not a cook book and it is not an instruction book for becoming a classically trained chef. This book represents the most useful of the cooking techniques and tricks that I picked up on my Food Pilgrimage travels. The tips come from the Restaurants of Italy and England, the home kitchens of Botswana and Peru, and the street carts of Vietnam and Morocco.

My hope is that they inspire you to go into the kitchen, unleash your creativity and wield your tools with more authority. These tips should make cooking easier and give you confidence. I want you to experiment, to impress and most importantly to enjoy life more through cooking for yourself and others.

So let's get cracking and get cooking.

Venice, 2012

Acknowledgements

The knowledge in this book was gleaned from the expertise of a host of gracious and talented cooks. I have simply compiled and translated it. While I have become quite adept in the kitchen, my passion for food is much more about getting you to cook and to bring people together. To this end, I rely on the shaman-like genius of the culinary magicians of the world and their willingness to share their mastery with me. Accordingly, any bad information is purely the fault of my translations.

The only virtue I can claim is a curious nature and having made the decision to set off to travel, seek out food and ask questions. Even in this, I was inspired by others. Here is but a brief list of gratitude.

Arrian Wheeler, who inspired me to gather people through feasts; Christy Marsh who changed the way I eat and travel; Jeanny Russell, who raised me at the kitchen island; Enrica Rocca, The Contessa of Venice, my indomitable Italian mentor; John Benbow of London's Food at 52, the most passionate and articulate cooking educator I know.

The kitchen staff and gracious cooks at countless restaurants that didn't even know they were inspiring me: Londra Palace, Venice; Borgo Bianco, Puglia; Falls of Dochart Inn, Killin; A Touch of Madness, Capetown; Da I due Ciccioni, Rome; About a zillion café owners and street vendors in Granada, Hanoi, Hoi-an, Lima, Ljubljana, Marrakesh, Maun, Saigon, Salamanca, Sarajevo… The list could go on forever.

Suffice it to say that I am grateful that the world is full of passionate food people willing to share through demonstration and inspiration.

Follow my weekly food adventures and learn about my cookery classes and food tours at

WWW.FOODPILGRIMAGE.COM

CONTENTS

Some Helpful Conversions

Wet (US Measures)

1 Tablespoon = 3 teaspoons = ½ fluid oz. = 15 ml

1 cup = 16 Tablespoons = 8 fluid oz. = 240 ml

1 pint = 2 cups = 480 ml

1 gallon = 4 quarts = 8 pints = 16 cups = 128 fluid oz. = 3.8L

100 ml = 6.7 Tablespoons (almost 1 Cup)

Dry

1 oz. = 28.4 grams

1 lb. = 16 oz. = 453 grams

100 grams = 3.5 oz.

1 kilogram = 2.2 pounds = 35 oz.

Dry Volume (approximations)

1 Tablespoon = 15 grams

1 cup = 240 grams

100 grams = about 6 US Tablespoons

Temperature

100 Celsius = 212 Fahrenheit

150 Celsius = 300 Fahrenheit

175 Celsius = 350 Fahrenheit

200 Celsius = 400 Fahrenheit

US to Imperial (UK)

1 US (t, T, Cup, quart, pint) = 0.83 Imperial

1 Imperial (t, T, Cup, quart, pint) = 1.2 US

The Chef's Knife: How to Hold it; How to Use it

The Chef's knife is the most important tool in the kitchen. Honing your knife skills will make cooking more fun, more efficient and much safer.

Hold the knife

Pinch the spine or bolster of the blade between thumb and fore-finger

Wrap remaining fingers loosely around the handle

Hold the food

Bend your wrist and arm 90 degrees

Tuck your thumb under your palm.

Curl back your fingertips

Guide the blade by resting the flat side against your index and middle finger knuckles

Slice

Anchor the nose of the knife on the cutting board, raising only the heel as needed.

Rock the knife forward in a single, smooth, controlled slicing motion.

Chef says

"Chopping is an unfortunate misnomer. The proper motion and technique is a relaxed, controlled slice. This slicing motion makes all the difference in ease, efficiency and safety."

THREE COCKTAILS TO KNOW BY HEART

Cocktail trends come and go, but the point of an evening aperitif is to relax, refresh and prepare your palate for the meal to come.

CHEF SAYS

"A cocktail should whet the appetite. Forget neon mystery mixes, umbrellas and wedges of fruit; dry, strong and cold are the order of the day. If you can turn out a perfected version of these classics, no one will ask for anything more."

THE OLD FASHIONED

Muddle **1t sugar, 3 dashes Angostura bitters** in an old fashioned glass. Add one lump of ice, **1 shot (about 50 ml)** of Top quality **Bourbon** or **blended whisky**, a **splash of soda** or water and a **twist of lemon peel**. Stir and serve.

THE DAIQUIRI

Muddle **2t sugar, 2T lime juice** in a highball glass. Add cubed ice to fill the glass, **1 shot of light rum**. Stir to frost the glass, and serve.

THE NEGRONI

Pour **1 shot dry gin, 1 shot sweet vermouth, and 1 shot Campari** over ice in an old fashioned glass. Stir, add a twist of **orange peel** and serve.

BISTRO STYLE STEAK

CHEF SAYS

"A good steak requires only a smoking hot cast-iron pan and a hot oven. A great steak requires a few finesse moves"

PREPARE

Place cast-iron pan in oven and Preheat to **500°F (260°C)**

Allow **steak** (1" to 1-¹/₂" sirloin, ribeye, T-bone, or rump) to come to room temperature.

Pat the steak dry.

Season both sides liberally with salt just before cooking.

Remove (exceptionally hot) pan from oven and place on stovetop over high heat.

Place steak directly onto dry pan.

Sear the steak for **1 minute** (without moving, poking or prodding) *(pg. 165)*

Flip and sear the other side for **1 minute** then place pan and steak directly in oven for **2 minutes**.

Flip steak and cook for additional **2 minutes** for a rare steak.

Test for desired doneness *(pg. 23)*

Remove steak from oven and pan and rest, undisturbed under a loose foil tent for **three minutes** before serving.

CRISPY PAN-FRIED FISH

Complexity has a way of ruining fish. Keep it simple. If you've got nine minutes and a hot pan, you can elevate salmon, trout, sea bass or any firm, skin-on fish to tender-fleshed, crispy-skinned, perfection; the pure expression of the fish.

PREPARE

Cut skin-on **fish fillets** to serving size.

Rest at room temperature and pat dry (Crucial for crispy skin).

Heat **2T oil** in heavy pan until nearly smoking.

Smear both sides of fish with **butter or oil.**

Season with **salt and pepper.**

Sear fish, skin-side down, until nearly cooked through (**3-5 minutes** per half-inch of thickness).

Flip and sear flesh side (**1-2 minutes**).

Present fish, skin side up, atop root vegetable puree *(pg. 153).*

CHEF SAYS

"Crispy skin means no more slippery, oily fish skin left on the plate. 80 percent of the cooking should happen while the skin side is down."

Poached Eggs

Poached eggs represent the pinnacle of egg expression. They are the centerpiece of numerous elevated brunch dishes. The secret to the Chef's poached egg is simple: A preliminary dunk, a soft touch, and vinegar.

Add **2T vinegar** to **1L of water** and bring to a rolling boil.

Reduce heat to a motionless simmer.

Plunge **whole, un-cracked egg** into the simmering water for **sixty seconds.**

Crack (slightly warm) egg into a small, shallow bowl (egg should be ever so slightly cloudy).

Gingerly pour egg from shallow bowl into center of simmering water.

Cook for two minutes.

Remove with a slotted spoon, drain excess water, then serve on grilled bread with hollandaise sauce (pg. 99)

Chef Says

"The extra time and effort spent poaching an egg turns common breakfast fare into something worthy of a champagne brunch"

Experiment

Eggs Florentine with spinach

Eggs Royale with smoked salmon

Eggs Benedict with smoked ham

Eggs Sardou with spicy sausage.

Silky-smooth Chocolate Ganache

The secret to a smooth, glossy ganache is a microwave and Butter. A double boiler is pretty, but risks adding moisture into the chocolate, which can cause it to split.

Prepare

In a glass bowl, place **7oz. (200g)** rough-chopped, top-quality **dark chocolate** (55-60% cocoa).

Microwave in **twenty-second** bursts, stirring between each, until smooth

Stir in **2T (30g) chopped cold butter** until melted through.

Stir in **6 oz. (180ml) heavy (double) cream** and $1/4$ t vanilla or $1/2$ T dark rum.

Experiment

by adding

1t grated **orange zest**

1t black **olive paste**

1 shot **espresso**

1T **Framboise** (raspberry liqueur) or **Grand Marnier** (orange liqueur)

Use as a tart filling, truffle paste, pastry filling... anywhere chocolate is welcome.

"THE MOST SOLID ADVICE ... IS THIS, I THINK...
REALLY TO TASTE FOOD WHEN YOU EAT... TRY AS
MUCH AS POSSIBLE TO BE WHOLLY ALIVE WITH ALL
YOUR MIGHT... YOU WILL BE DEAD SOON
ENOUGH."

~ ERNEST HEMINGWAY

White-Wine, Lemon-Butter pan Sauce

Guests are amazed when the Chef pulls this silky, rich sauce out of thin air. The Chef loves it as it requires only three ingredients that are always in the pantry. The Chef uses this on flaky fish, fowl, and mild game, like rabbit.

Pan sear and cook through your fish, game or fowl and remove from pan.

Deglaze the pan with **4T white wine**, heating through to burn off the alcohol.

Off of the heat, add **2t lemon zest, juice of one lemon, 2T unsalted butter.**

Whisk to incorporate, season to taste, multiply recipe as needed.

Pour over fish or meat just before serving.

Experiment

by adding

1T chopped shallot, 1T mustard, or 1T caper buds

¹/₄ t fresh dill, marjoram or tarragon

¹/₂ t crushed green peppercorns

.

OVEN ROASTED VEGETABLES

Shopping seasonally means making the most of whatever the garden gives you. This technique takes zero prep and lends a caramelized sweetness to sturdy vegetables like turnips, beets, sweet potatoes and carrots. It also works wonders on squash, green beans, broccoli and asparagus.

CHEF SAYS

"Getting a good caramelized roast on vegetables transforms them into sweet, crisp goodness."

PREPARE

Preheat oven to 450°F (230°C)

Slice **1 lb. vegetables** into ¼" thick half-moons, or 1" cubes.

Toss with **4T olive oil** and season liberally with **salt**.

Arrange on a sheet pan in a single layer.

Roast until browned (**20 to 40 minutes** depending on the vegetable) tossing occasionally.

Toss with additional **olive oil**, **salt and pepper** to taste.

Turn out onto serving platter.

EXPERIMENT

Add another flavor layer buy tossing uncooked vegetables with 1T of lemon zest, chopped garlic, chopped shallot, chopped marjoram or chopped rosemary.

or

Toss roasted vegetables with chopped chives, torn basil, or grated parmesan or pecorino cheese.

21

Know When Meat is Done

Chef Says

"No matter how comfortable I get with cooking meat, I touch it to test doneness. The difference between medium-rare and medium may be only seconds, but the remorse of an overcooked steak can last a lifetime."

The Technique

Touch the tip of your **thumb** to the tip of your **finger** (touch, don't press). Poke the fleshy part of the base of your thumb as the reference point.

Thumb to index finger is the firmness of a **raw** cut.

Thumb to middle finger is **medium-rare** (the most commonly requested "doneness").

Thumb to ring finger is **medium.**

Thumb to pinky is **well-done** (ruined).

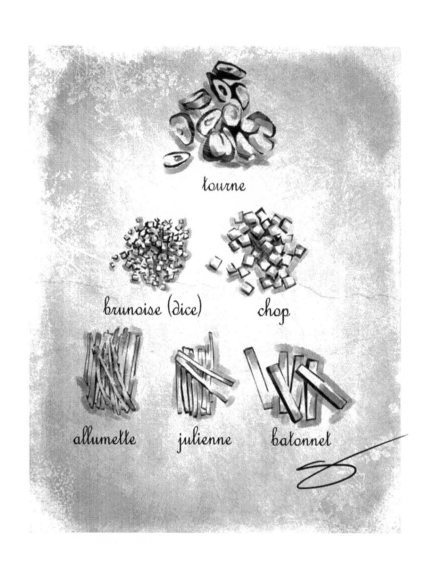

tourne

brunoise (dice) chop

allumette julienne batonnet

Chopping Shapes that Matter.

Culinary academies love to dazzle with their curiously named and complicated array of food shapes.

Chef Says

"Slices, then sticks then pieces. Ninety-five percent of my dishes rely on these steps. The variation is in the size."

Batonet: Thick sticks about $1/2$" x $1/2$" x 2"

Allumette (matchstick): Thin sticks about $1/4$" x $1/4$" x 2"

Julienne: Very thin sticks about $1/8$" x $1/8$" by 2 inches

Cube: Uniform pieces about 1" x 1" x 1"

Chop: Uniform pieces about $1/2$" x $1/2$"

Brunoise: Uniform pieces about $1/4$" x $1/4$"

Mince: Non-uniform fine cut about the size of a grain of rice.

If you've got the time and the energy, impress your friends by learning these:

Tourne ("turned" and cut into an oblong)

Rondelle (round slice)

Paysanne ("peasant style" thin slices)

Lozenge (fancy diamond shape)

Fermiere (rustic "farmer" slice)

Chiffonade: leafy herbs rolled tightly and cut into thin ribbons

The key to mastering any of these shapes is in choosing the right, sharp knife and holding the knife correctly *(pg. 5)*.

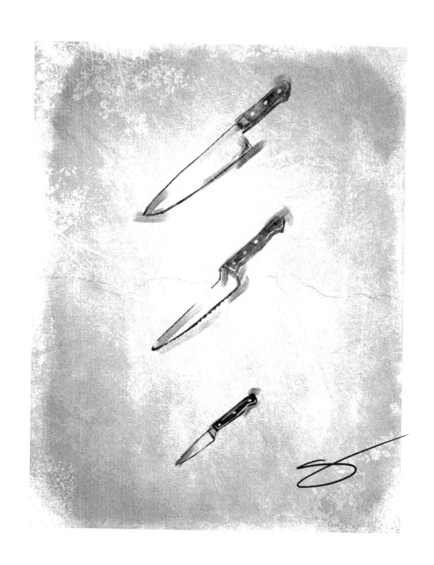

THE ONLY THREE KNIVES THE CHEF NEEDS

Forget the knife block, the drawer of specialty blades and the trendy Japanese daggers and Toledo swords. The chef cuts many things in a day, and uses only these three knives. He sharpens them regularly.

THE 9" (20 CM) CHEF'S CHOPPING KNIFE

Chop, core, slice, dice, even bone and fillet. The workhorse that should feel like your best friend.

THE PARING KNIFE OR UTILITY KNIFE

Scrape, core, peel and pare. This is the tool for close up work off of the cutting board.

THE OFFSET SERRATED BLADE

For the specialty jobs: slicing hard bread, soft tomatoes and anything fibrous.

When your kitchen gets fancy you may earn the right to procure a flexible boning knife for game and fish, but make sure you have a real reason.

CHEF SAYS

"Next time you're considering a kitchen gift for a friend; forget the garlic masher, the fancy wine opener or any other one-trick gadget. Get them one, quality chef's knife that they can pass on to their children."

Brilliant Béchamel

At its simplest, béchamel is simply flour, butter and milk.

Yet, mastering béchamel unlocks a realm of rich and satisfying dishes.

Chef Says

"Many great dishes depend on the silky, smooth richness of this most simple of sauces."

In a large, heavy sauce pan, heat **5T butter** over medium heat until foamy.

Whisk in **4T flour** until smooth and cook (whisking constantly) until lightly golden.

Add **3C milk (750ml)**, **1C (250ml)** at a time, whisking until smooth.

Heat just to a boil (sauce will thicken rapidly) and immediately reduce heat to low. Simmer over low heat stirring occasionally for **10 minutes**.

Season with **salt** and a pinch of **nutmeg**.

Set aside for use as a sauce base or for a vegetable or pasta bake.

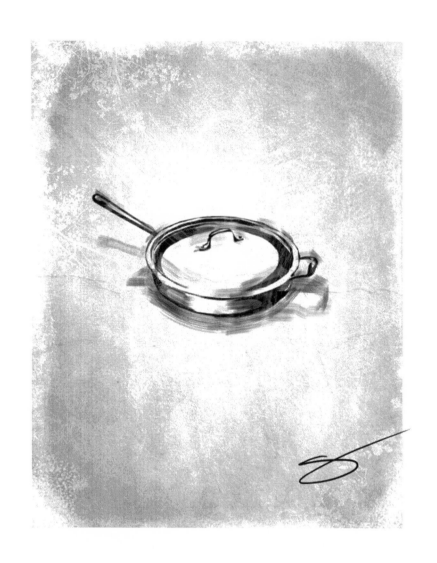

The Cook's Pans

Every kitchen needs at least one Cast Iron pan and one Non-stick pan.

The Cast-iron Pan

Heat to high and wipe with butter or oil for searing meat and browning crusts onto starches or vegetables.

Wipe clean and never wash with soap or water.

The Non-stick Pan

Heat to medium for eggs, cheese and sticky starches like fried polenta.

Wipe clean. Never scour or scrub.

Heavy Sauté Pan

Everything else goes in a heavy-bottomed sauté pan; stainless steel or copper-clad if you're fancy. High heat and oil will keep most foods from sticking.

Chef Says

"Cookware made only of copper is really only for decorating the pot-rack."

Tagines in the Medina

My memorable Marrakesh meal was had by chance while wandering stray, down a narrow alley, having missed my riad by one street. I wasn't really hungry for a meal, but the stray-toothed grin of a lanky local in a chef's blouse laboring over a row of sizzling meat skewers, and the presence of numerous robed men in white beards hunched over bowls of soup and thick bread (and the lack of a menu) was enough to convince me that this was an establishment to be embraced.

My French is pretty bad and my Arabic is non-existent, so the majority of my communicating with the chef was done via gesture. This suited me fine as all of the available food stuffs were on display and could be easily pointed to. Most were careful renditions of Marrakesh street food staples: There were the skewered lamb liver and kidney pierced alongside charred cubes of leg and shoulder, sizzling and streaked with black grill marks. There were the tall silver stew-pots with their pungent mixes of beans and deep red spices, and there were the ubiquitous tagines, lined up like clay soldiers waiting for inspection; little puffs of vapor leaking from under the cone covers. After pointing excitedly at a number of the various food vessels, I retired to take my place in a plastic chair in the sun to wait and see what the chef made of my wild gestures.

The beans came out first, in a thick sauce of paprika and turmeric; deep orange, creamy and hearty. The second dish was a plate of small fish, each about the size of a child's hand, folded over, and fried, pressed as they cook so that they came out thin and crispy. The fish were served with a cooling sauce of vinegar and mint. The meat dish was an oily stew of slow cooked shoulder pieces and toasted turmeric and star anise that gave the dish a warm, Christmas flavor. The Meat yielded at the slightest touch and could be eaten with only a fork.

After a second plate of the fried fish, I sat back and felt the line of the shade move over me as the sun slipped behind the flimsy market stall awnings. From the long metal table of fires and grills, the chef would shout over and draw my attention to whatever dish he was serving up or whatever skewered meat he had just taken off the flames. He saw that I was into my food and new that he had his fan club for the afternoon.

Marrakesh, 2011

How to Handle Garlic

Rustic

Garlic can simply be crushed with the flat blade of a chef's knife. The skin will pull away fairly easily and the garlic is ready for slicing, rough chopping or adding whole.

Fancy

Cut off the dry woody end of the garlic clove and then cut lengthwise. The skin will simply fall away.

If the core has a green shoot, pull this out. This fibrous cellulose is the source of bitter taste and bad breath.

Slice, chop or mash as needed.

The Classic Tomato Sauce

The secret to velvety, rich tomato sauce is a little bit of time, and a whole lot of butter or oil. (Hey, it feeds a whole family)

Prepare

In a medium sauce pan combine **4T butter** or **4T Olive oil, 1 (20 oz.) tin of San Marzano tomatoes, 2 cloves smashed garlic, 1 yellow-onion** halved, (but not sliced or chopped).

Simmer for **one hour** over medium-low heat.

Remove the onion and garlic.

Cook ½ lb. of good, dry pasta, just shy of al-dente.

Combine sauce and drained pasta over heat to incorporate *(pg. 145)*.

Serve with an inky black Nebiolo wine to transport yourself to sunny southern Italy.

START BY SEARING IT

The chef unlocks the true potential of meat (and vegetables) by searing a healthy brown crust through undisturbed heating. This develops complex flavors through a reaction of proteins and fats or sugars.

CHEF SAYS

"Developing a proper seared crust through browning requires nothing more than high heat and patience. It is a discerning discipline of the seasoned cook."

PREPARE

Allow meat to come to room temperature

Pat dry

Season liberally just prior to cooking

Add a film of **oil, butter, or fat** to a very hot pan

Place ingredients in single layer

Allow to **sear, undisturbed for 1-5 minutes,** peaking only at edges for a healthy brown crust. Flip and repeat.

"No shifting, no shaking, no cutting and no stabbing. Learn to gauge browning success by smell, sound and intuition."

Perfect your Vinaigrette

Vinaigrettes are stellar do-all sauces that require no recipes, only a formula

Starting with **1T acid,** slowly whisk in **3-4T oil.**

Encourage emulsification and add some bite by adding ½ t **mustard or horseradish.**

Multiply as needed.

Use on salad greens, steamed vegetables, roasted potatoes, as a dipping sauce, or as a marinade for meat, fish and fowl.

Chef Says

"The magic lies in allowing your ingredients - local and seasonal - to inspire your sauce."

Experiment

Try these combinations:

Champagne vinegar and walnut oil

Balsamic vinegar and fruity (extra-virgin) olive oil

Rice wine vinegar and toasted sesame oil

Fresh Lemon juice and light olive oil

Experiment

Take the sauce to the next level by adding **1T** of any of the following:

Fresh chopped basil, thyme, marjoram, shallot or garlic.

And don't forget to season with salt and pepper to taste

STACK IT IN A RING MOLD

Most things look better (and therefore taste better) when presented tall.

The best tool for accomplishing this is an eye and palate pleasing ring mold. Use this device to layer ingredients, keeping flavors and colors distinct. This works especially well for **tar-tares, chopped salads** and **ceviches**.

PREPARE

Wipe inside surface of ring mold with neutral oil and place on a clean plate.

Stack ingredients in distinct layers.

Carefully remove ring mold and finish the stack with a dash of bottle sauce *(pg. 81)*

CHEF SAYS

"There is something ethereal and angelic about a tall cylinder of exquisite ingredients in the middle of a clean, white plate."

44

Simple, Vibrant, Cooked Vegetables

Banish the stigma of mushy, bland vegetables. The chef uses this technique to get vegetables to the table fast, fresh, flavorful and intact. Quick sautéing in oil keeps the vegetables bright and crisp. The dash of liquid at the end adds the perfect amount of steam as a finale.

This works brilliantly with broccoli, green beans, asparagus, baby carrots, and hard greens like kale, chard and collards.

Prepare

Heat **3T olive oil** in heavy bottom sauté pan over medium heat.

Add **1/2 pound chopped, sliced or julienned vegetables, 2 cloves sliced garlic** and **zest of 1 lemon.** Cook for **5-8 minutes,** tossing constantly, until slightly softened. Add **juice of 1 lemon** or **2T white wine** or **2T wine vinegar** and cook an additional 1 minute or until liquid thickens and vegetables reach desired tenderness.

Season with **salt and pepper,** turn out onto serving platter and drizzle with **additional oil.**

Experiment

Add a dash of dried red chili flakes, or a sprinkling of Parmigiano Reggiano cheese to finish.

"Every opportunity to nourish oneself with food can become a pilgrimage when the dreaming, planning, seeking out, preparing and consuming of that food is pursued with passion, and enthusiasm"

~ The Original Food Pilgrimage Motto

STOCK WITH PERSONALITY

There is no substitute for the heartiness of home-made stock. Anytime you are in possession of animal bones, you owe it to yourself to make stock.

PREPARE

In a large, heavy-bottomed stock pot, heat **4T oil** and **sauté the flavor base** (Chicken carcass, beef or lamb bones, fish bones, prawn shells) till browned and fragrant (**about 5 minutes**).

Add **1 onion** (cut into halves), **2 rough-cut carrots**, **2 stalks celery**, **4 cloves smashed garlic**, and a **bouquet garnis** of thyme sprigs, sage leaves, rosemary sprigs and bay leaf.

EXPERIMENT

with other flavor additions:

clove, star anise, celery seed, fennel seed.

Fill pot with **cold water** and simmer for up to **4 hours** (**only 30 minutes for fish stock**).

Skim off fat, strain, divide and store (refrigerate for up to a week, freeze for up to two months)

CHEF SAYS

"Leave stock unseasoned. Add salt only when preparing the final dish. (Adding salt to sauces and stocks can lead to over-seasoning as they reduce and concentrate)"

THE HAMBURGER

The chef cooks a burger only one way.

The perfect burger is not flame-broiled; it is not char-grilled; it is not barbecued. The perfect burger is cooked on a hot pan or flat griddle, much like the perfect steak *(pg. 9)*.

CHEF SAYS

"Like so many meats, the burger is at its best when it is seared, and allowed to cook in its own fat."

Stir ¼ t salt into **2lb ground chuck** or **brisket.**

Shape into **four ½" thick patties.**

Season both sides of each patty with additional **salt.**

Heat a cast iron skillet over high heat.

Wipe pan with a thin film of **butter or oil**

Grill patties, undisturbed for **3-4 minutes** on one side.

Flip and grill for **2-3 minutes** for rare, 2 additional minutes for medium-rare.

Allow cooked burger to rest for **3 minutes** *(pg. 165)*

Serve on a **soft bun** that has been toasted, face-down on the pan for 30 seconds.

CHEF SAYS

"Stir and handle the meat as little as possible. Handling melts valuable fat and renders a tough burger.)

Consider serving with one of many complimentary condiments other than ketchup."

EXPERIMENT

Top with sautéed onion, crispy bacon, mature cheddar cheese, garlic aioli *(pg. 137)*, or Chimichurri. *(pg. 119)*

Rice two Ways

There is perfect rice, and there is very-fast, nearly perfect rice. Both have their purposes. The deciding factor is how much time you want to spend with your guests.

Well-cooked rice is fluffy, with each grain separate. There is no excuse for watery, mushy, sticky or scalded rice.

Perfect steamed rice

The science is in the steaming.

Combine **2C (480g) Rice, 1t light oil** and **4C (960ml) Water** in a heavy sauce pan

Bring to a boil.

Immediately reduce heat to low.

Cover and simmer, for **15 minutes.**

Fluff and serve.

Nearly perfect fast rice

Treat the rice like pasta.

Bring **8C (about 2 litres) Water** to a boil in a heavy sauce pan.

Add **2C (480g) rice, 2t salt** and boil until tender (about **10 minutes**)

Drain in a fine colander.

Chef Says

"Only if you find yourself making rice three times a day, is it time to get a proper rice cooker."

BOILED EGGS

The perfect boiled egg is a dish of luxury on its own.

Perfection lies in the yolk; not runny, but far from the chalky gray that results from shock and overcooking.

The yolk should be golden and soft at the core and pale yellow at the edge.

PREPARE

Place **2-6 eggs** in a sauce pan and cover with **cold water** and **1T vinegar**. Bring to a simmer over high heat. As soon as the water bubbles, remove pan from heat, and let sit for **7-9 minutes** (experiment for your elevation and taste).

Drain and refresh in **cold water** to ensure shells slide off effortlessly.

Peel, chop and add to a Niçoise salad, crumble on top of gazpacho, or simply spread on toast.

Sautéed Mushrooms

Whether foraged in the wild or picked up at the local farmers market, mushrooms deserve exquisite preparation. Luckily, this is universally easy.

Remember

Raw mushrooms soak up oil, water and everything else they contact.

Don't overcrowd the sauté pan (this leads to steaming).

Mushrooms reduce by two-thirds when cooked down

If your guests don't like mushrooms, they're not your real friends.

Wipe a large, dry sauté pan and with a **thin film of butter or oil** and heat until nearly smoking.

Add **sliced or quartered mushrooms**.

Sauté until thoroughly browned (**4-6 minutes**), then flip.

Once browned and reduced, stir in a **pat of butter or glug of oil** and **a few drops of lemon juice and a few drops of water**.

Experiment

Stir in 1T chopped shallot or 1t chopped tarragon.

To create a saucier finish, add 1t of flour, heat through and whisk in 1T of white wine, sherry vinegar or water.

For the ultimate pure mushroom experience, serve on crusty grilled bread with finishing oil and salt

Don't Salt the Water

When boiling or steaming grains and beans into soup, porridge, risotto or pilaf, avoid salting your broth, stock or boiling water.

Chef Says

"Salted water will render grains and legumes that are tough and pulses that are soupy. Salt toughens the outer skin, inhibiting water absorption and starch development.

Season to taste once the grains or beans are cooked and creamy.

60

LOVELY LEAFY GREENS

Nearly every food culture on the planet integrates bitter greens into cuisine. Most often used as an appetizer, bitter foods whet the appetite and cleanse the palate. Dive deeper than mere spinach.

EXPERIMENT

Mix any of these **raw greens** into lettuces to add bite and brightness to a salad.

frisse

radicchio

chicory

endive

escarole

Hard greens in these families shine from simple pan sauté preparation *(pg. 45)*.

chard

kale

mustard, turnip or collard greens

CHEF SAYS

"Bitter flavors are a key component of the taste spectrum. Too often, cuisine relies on salty and sweet and occasionally sour. Bitter flavors add a whole new dimension to the complete meal experience"

A Café Table in Spain

In the morning, on the Boulevard in Granada, the wicker café seats are all full by the time the sun reaches over the Teatro Isabel. No matter how hot the day will become, this early, the sun is welcome. The chat is relaxed because anyone sitting out at the marble topped tables is not going in to work that day and so has time to solve the world's problems.

The breakfast in front of each person is the same. Probably the same every day that they are sat here: A heavy, white plate with two browned halves of crusty bread. On the bread is a thin smear of clean, crushed tomato; fresh if it is August, from a glass jar, if it is not. On the layer of tomato, goes salt, and on top of the salt, is poured out a puddle of olive oil from a metal tin can, not much different from an old oil-can for lubricating farm machinery. The oil even makes the tic-tic sound as it is poured out. The whole assembly rests; the tomato and oil seeping downward, into the rough surface of the toasted bread. Next to the plate is a small glass of fresh squeezed orange juice that is made to order at a counter-top machine with gears and belts that sounds like a drill press. The juice has tart pulp on the top and is thinner and more refreshing at the bottom of the glass.

If you are a journalist, or an activist, you have coffee instead of juice. The coffee is served in a clear glass; a double shot from a giant chrome espresso machine cut with hot milk poured in from a metal pitcher brought out to your table

This meager breakfast can be stretched through conversation and savoring to last hours. In Spain, it is a well-regarded art form to labor and extend the enjoyment of a café breakfast. If you sit long enough to watch the sun move behind the tall, cream-colored, Hotel Juan Miguel, you will see old men in flat caps order short, fat glasses of cold beer. And because this is Granada, these come with bread and ham and olives, and just like that; lunch is happening.

Then will come the Africans, spreading out their flimsy canvas blankets to sell leather belts and purses, always with one as the look-out, and there will be well-dressed families out for a lunch-time stroll, the small boys with matching wool vests, winding string around old fashioned tops.

This is every day in Granada, and most other towns in Spain. Sleepy or bustling, festival or workday, there is always an open chair and table on the sidewalk and you are always welcome to take your time

Granada, 2011.

Olive Oil and Black Pepper to Finish

Anything simple and savory looks and tastes better finished with a drizzle of vivid green or golden oil and a twist of cracked black pepper.

Chef Says

"This simple finishing makes the food look like it just jumped off the page of a glossy food magazine."

Exceptional aesthetic candidates

egg dishes

antipasto or appetizer plates

thick soups

sautéed vegetables

salad greens

dips and spreads

grilled fish and fowl

Fish in a Parcel

There are a million ways to cook fish. But this one requires no supervision, and yields tender fish and crisp vegetables with plenty of flavor.

Prepare

Fold tinfoil or parchment into a vapor tight envelope, longer and much wider than the fish.

In the envelope, combine **1 lb. Fish steaks**, fillets or whole fish patted dry and seasoned with **salt and pepper, 1C (240g) Thin-sliced (1/8 in.) or julienned vegetables, 3T white wine, sherry or vermouth**

Aromatics

Roll open end to seal and bake at **375°F (190°C) for 20-30 minutes.** Cut envelope open, season additionally and serve.

Experiment

3 cloves smashed **garlic**, half a **lemon**, half an **onion**, half a **fennel** bulb (all sliced thin) and 5 sprigs fresh **dill**, 3T dry **white wine.**

or

2 **star anise** pods, 5 ground **cloves**, 1/2 t ground **coriander seed**, 1 carrot, half an **orange** (both sliced thin), 3T dry **vermouth.**

or

2 cloves smashed **garlic**, 1 **lime**, half a **tomato** (both sliced thin), 1T Asian **fish sauce**, 1T red **chili flakes** or Thai curry paste, 3T **chopped cilantro** (coriander leaf), 3T **rice wine vinegar.**

Chef Says

"There is something grandiose and impressive about food in a package. The whole table is impressed when you poke into the parcel, releasing a gasp of steam and fragrance."

THE CITRUS JUICER

Commonly found in the hands of very capable Latin American chefs (and who uses more citrus?), the simple lever juicer is the first and last you will ever need. Take pride when you finally wear the paint off of yours.

CHEF SAYS

Forget the glass juicer, the electric juicer or the two-foot tall bolt-on counter top affair. Procure one of these sturdy metal hand-held devices and dive in to a lemon pan sauce *(pg. 19)* or vinaigrette *(pg. 41)*

DREDGING FOR A CRISP CRUST

CHEF SAYS

"Few kitchen sounds area as appetizing as setting the perfectly coated food into hot oil. The question of oil, timing and temperature can be debated, but perfect crusts all have similar roots."

PREPARE

Pat your meat or vegetables dry.

Set up a dredging station of three bowls.

DRY COAT

corn starch, wheat flour or baking powder

WET COAT

milk, buttermilk, or egg

CRUST COAT

fresh or dried bread crumbs, panko crumbs, herbed flour or cornstarch (Seasoned to taste)

Use one hand to drag the food through the dry and set into the wet. Use the other hand to transfer from the wet to the crust. Return to the dry hand to transfer the food to plate for pan frying or deep frying.

Roux and Gravy

Roux is simply some kind of fat heated through with a starch (usually all-purpose flour). The resulting paste acts as a thickening agent when heated through in sauces, soups or stews.

It is a fundamental tool in the Chef's bag of tricks.

Simply add roux to stock (pg. 49) to make the perfect gravy.

Prepare Roux

Heat

4T fat (Butter, lard or drippings) over medium-high heat until melted or foaming.

Add **4T all-purpose flour,** whisking vigorously. Reduce heat to low. Cook until bubbles form and the mixture is thickened and smells toasty.

This quantity will thicken 4 Cups (nearly a litre) of liquid.

Chef says

"To avoid lumps, temper the finished roux into what you are thickening: Add 4T of the liquid to the roux, whisk vigorously. Then add that mixture back into your liquid"

The thickening power of the roux kicks in only when the roux and liquid are heated through, together, to a near-boil.

The Sweetness of Balsamic Glaze

The Chef always has this rich, sweet reduction on hand. It takes no special ingredients, just a little planning. It's not "Tradizionale", but it is true nobility when compared to a simple wine vinegar drizzle.

Use this to add a rich, sweet tang to roasted game, fowl, roasted or sautéed vegetables, even fresh or grilled seasonal fruit.

Prepare

In a heavy bottomed sauce pan, combine

2C (480ml) balsamic vinegar with **1C (240g) sugar or 2C (480ml) of cloudy apple juice.**

Simmer (uncovered) over low heat until reduced by half and bubbles become slightly thick

Drizzle over finished dish.

or

Cool and store in a plastic squeeze bottle. *(pg. 81)*

Experiment

Add flavor layers with any of the following while cooking down. (Remove before serving)

1 sprig rosemary

zest strips of 1 orange

1T green peppercorns

1T chopped shallot

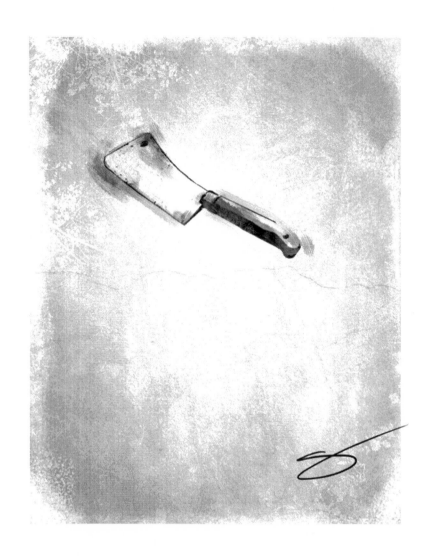

"ONE OF THE VERY NICEST THINGS ABOUT LIFE
IS THE WAY WE MUST REGULARLY STOP WHATEVER
IT IS WE ARE DOING AND DEVOTE OUR
ATTENTION TO EATING."

~LUCIANO PAVAROTTI

Sauce Artistry

The Chef keeps plastic, screw-top squeeze-bottles of a variety of finishing sauces within reach.

Chef Says

"A good looking plate shows attention to detail and allows the eyes to indulge before the dish is tasted. A few dashes of color can hint at the flavours to come."

Apply in spirals, circles or dots as a bed or a finish. For added flair, flatten some shapes with the back of a spoon or drag through with a toothpick.

Good candidates

garlic aioli *(pg. 137)*

green, herby vinaigrette *(pg. 41)*

balsamic glaze *(pg. 77)*

crème Fresh

red berry coulis

chocolate sauce

A Touch of Coffee in Chocolate Deserts

Chocolate mousse, chocolate ganache, chocolate cake... Any molten chocolate based desert gets a shot of strongly brewed coffee or espresso in the mix.

Chef says

"The earthiness and pungency add depth and sophistication to the dish and keep it from becoming cloyingly sweet...And don't forget to season (pg. 93)"

The Scrambled Egg

The perfect scrambled egg is a 3-minute affair requiring only a pan, a spatula, and good butter.

Heat **1T unsalted butter** in a non-stick pan over medium heat until foam subsides.

Crack **2 eggs** directly into pan.

Push and swirl with a spatula until streaky, but not fully scrambled. Heat through until creamy, but not quite dry.

Turn out onto a plate and season with a pinch of salt and a twist of pepper.

If the chef adds vegetables, cheese or meat, those ingredients are cooked through in a separate pan and added to the eggs halfway through cooking.

Chef Says

"Scrambled eggs should be soft with the rich flavor and color of yolk marbled throughout.

Cooking too long makes eggs rubbery.

Adding salt prior to cooking makes eggs grainy.

Adding water or milk makes eggs too fluffy."

Pesto Any Which Way

Full of color and flavor, Pestos can be made out of nearly anything. They pair well with pasta, grilled meat, crudité, and salads. Pestos are never cooked. Experiment with ingredients from a single region.

Prepare

3 handfuls loose, leafy herbs

3T grated hard, aged, sharp cheese

3T lightly toasted tree nuts

1t - 2T flavor component

Oil to bind (about 6T) and salt to taste (About ¼ t)

Blend first four ingredients in a small food processor or mortar and pestle until finely chopped and well combined. Gradually drizzle in oil to an oozing consistency and season to taste.

Experiment with Herbs

basil, parsley, arugula (rocket), watercress, cilantro (coriander), mint, nettles

Experiment with Cheese

parmesan, pecorino, mahon, aged gruyere, dry feta

Experiment with Nuts

pine nuts, walnuts, skinned almonds, hazelnuts (filberts)

Experiment with Flavour Components

peeled garlic, sun-dried tomato, roasted red peppers, lemon zest, cured olives

Experiment with Oil

olive oil, walnut oil, toasted sesame seed oil, grape seed oil

A Stack of Kitchen Towels

Chef says

"You can never have too many neatly-folded, clean kitchen towels stacked up next to your cooking area."

The world over, you will see seasoned home cooks, line-cooks and street food vendors rely on these to handle pots, wipe plates, and dry hands.

BOIL A LOBSTER

Guests love lobster and mediocre cooks love to ruin lobster by smothering, smashing and stuffing it.

Good lobster should be boiled, and then eaten.

Ask your fishmonger for **one good 2-4 lb. live, female, hard-shell lobster**

Drop head first into heavily-salted, boiling water

Cover and boil: 7 minutes per pound plus 4 minutes.

Remove, pat dry, split body lengthwise, crack claws and consume.

CHEF SAYS

"Drawn butter is optional, anything additional is abuse."

Season your Sweets

Salt has just as much flavour opening impact in deserts as it does in savory dishes. The chef always adds a pinch to cake batters, tart crusts, mousses and ganaches.

Some deserts like chocolate and custards even benefit from a pinch of finishing salt just before serving.

Chef Says

"The quantity of salt may be small, but the effect is important. Salt awakens the tongue; as true for pastry as it is for potatoes. Experiment by adding one pinch at a time"

A Fish Shack in Africa

In a dusty parking lot in Maun, Botswana, there is a tiny shack that only sells one thing. It is tucked in behind a repair garage. The door is a beaded curtain, the walls are peeling plaster and the roof is corrugated sheet metal. Garlicky smoke lifts up from a hole cut in the peak. No hawkers yell out to you, no touts drag you over. The casual observer will see the odd local walk by, lay a few coins and walk away with a non-descript white box.

If you see this place, you should eat here. You should order the only thing they offer.

That one thing is a fresh river fish, caught this morning and fried whole in a shallow pan full of oil. The fish is scored and cut so that it cooks evenly and can be picked apart with bare fingers. There are no condiments offered, so one can assume none are needed. The Appropriate accompanying beverage is an exceptionally strong ginger beer served in one of those scuffed, thick glass bottles.

The key to the one item shack is that it leaves no room for the artisan to be anything other than a master of the one item. No special "value meal deals" to lure you in, no up-selling or super-sizing. The vendor will tell you everything about the food in a passionate patter with the crazed look of an obsessed deep-sea treasure hunter. The guy knows where the ingredients came from, he's tried a zillion recipe variations and he knows what keeps his customers happy.

When traveling, I think of how many dining establishments are concocted for the vagrant masses; the outsiders who will be in town for exactly as long as it takes to find a cash-machine and get lunch. These places know that you will not be a repeat visitor regardless of their culinary effort and dedication. As long as they can lure you in, they'll make the one sale. I think of the single item shack as the opposite and consider it one of the greatest ways to create an unforgettable food experience in any town regardless of time constraints. Without these quick incursions into local territory, every city is just another Starbuck's, McDonald's, or Nando's that washes into the bucket of non-descript travel memories.

Sights, sounds and photo opportunities can all blur together. Even memorable meals can become jumbled. The single item shack stands out because it has such a singular place in existence. This one fried fish will forever hold the key to a deluge of memories that lead up to and follow the procurement and eating of it. I love that.

You should go seek out this shack. It can be found anywhere. Back in San Diego it would be slinging street tacos, in Bosnia it was sausages and onions, in Spain would be fried Churros and thick drinking chocolate. First world, Third world, somewhere, somebody has perfected one thing and has a dedicated following that you should become a part of. Ask around or think back to the one you saw last week, grab a friend and make it your next Food Pilgrimage.

Maun Botswana, 2011

The Luxury Sauces: Hollandaise and Béarnaise

Useful for a number of rich decadent dishes, Hollandaise sauce is simple in its ingredients if a little tedious in its preparation

Chef says

"Mastery of this family of sauces unlocks a host of decadent dishes."

Prepare Hollandaise

Gently heat **2T white vinegar** and ¹/₂ t **white pepper** until reduced by half

Drizzle reduction (while whisking) into **2 large, beaten egg yolks.**

Gently heat mixture over a double boiler, whisking constantly until mixture triples in volume.

Remove from heat and drizzle in (while whisking) **3/4C (180g) melted unsalted butter** until thickened and velvety

Whisk in **2t lemon juice**, salt and pepper to taste

Ladle while warm over fish, eggs, asparagus, broccoli or cooked greens.

For Sauce Béarnaise

Substitute the vinegar mixture above with:

4T wine vinegar, 4T white wine, 1T minced shallot, 1T fresh tarragon, ¹/₄ t white pepper.

Heat gently until reduced by half and drizzle into egg and add butter as above (skip the lemon).

Ladle Béarnaise over heartier fare, like poultry, game and steaks.

100

Cook With Wine you Would Drink

Anything labeled cooking wine, cooking sherry or cooking Marsala has no place in the kitchen.

Add to a dish, only that which you would drink (ideally, that which you *will* drink).

Chef says

"Any dish worthy of eating is worthy of wine that is worthy of drinking.

Consider that wine and spirits only get further reduced and concentrated as you cook them down. This means that the good, or bad qualities get amplified.

...and never underestimate the nuance of a regional dish that can be captured by adding alcohol authentic to the region."

Potatoes: Baked, Roasted, Mashed, Fried

Among The Chef's favorite dishes is the humble potato, cooked to perfection, paired with fresh butter. Master these four basic ways to prepare a potato.

The Baked potato

Rub **oil and sea salt** onto a **starchy potato** (Russet, Piper or King Edward). Prick liberally with a fork and place in pre-heated **400°F (200°C)** Oven for **1 – 1.5 hours** (until golden, crispy and tender when squeezed). Split, dress and serve.

The Roast Potato

Peel and boil small (chicken egg sized), **waxy potatoes** (New, Fingerling, or Red) in **salted water** for **6-9 minutes**. Drain and dry. Rub with **fat** (butter, oil, duck fat), **season** and roast in pre-heated **350°F (175°C)** oven for **40-60 minutes**, tossing at 20 minute intervals. Toss and serve.

The Mashed Potato

Peel, split and boil **starchy potatoes** in **salted water** until fork tender, but not crumbly (about **15 minutes**). Drain, dry and mash with **4T milk or cream**, **4T butter or oil**. Stir in additional flavors *(pg. 153)*, season and serve.

The Skillet-Fried Potato

Peel, half and thinly (1/4") slice **starchy potatoes**. Season and cook in **2T oil** in heavy skillet (covered) over medium heat for **10 minutes** (until browned and crisp). Add **2T additional oil**. Flip and cook **7-10 minutes** more (covered). Toss and flip again. Stir in additional flavors, cook uncovered for **5 minutes**. Season and serve.

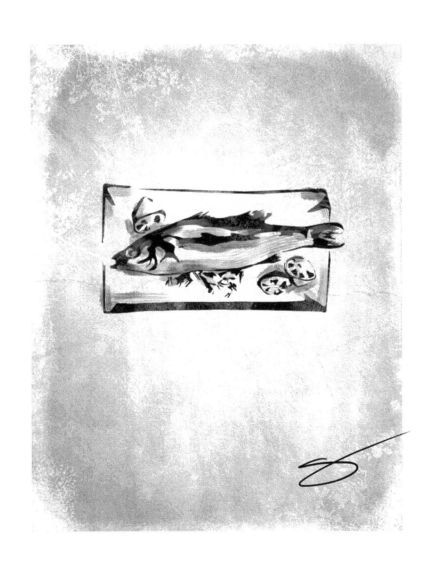

FILLET A WHOLE, COOKED FISH

CHEF SAYS

"What good is the majesty of a whole cooked fish if one butchers the beast in trying to eat it?"

Fileting a fresh, raw fish is a task for practice, but anyone can master the simple deconstruction of a whole cooked fish.

Don't fuss with removing the head or the tail.

PREPARE

Lay cooked, steamed, grilled or roasted whole fish onto a flat serving platter. Pull away any fins from top or bottom.

With a fork or fingers, hold the fish stationary by the tail end.

Starting at the tail, **push** along the spine in one long, smooth motion with a fish knife or other dull blade, working towards the head to separate and remove the fillet in one piece.

Lift the spine by the tail, keeping the bottom filet stationary with a fork.

Remove the soft pin-bones from the meaty area at the wide end of the filets.

Arrange the two fillet halves on a plate. Drizzle with **lemon-butter** *(pg. 19)* or another appropriate sauce *(pg. 41)* and serve.

Season the Water

The Chef heavily seasons the cooking water when cooking pasta, poaching fish and meat, or when boiling or blanching vegetables.

Chef Says

"The cooking process is a crucial opportunity to impart seasoning into these dishes."

Pasta comes alive. Fish and meat pick up depth of flavor and vegetables stay vibrant.

Add **1t kosher salt or sea-salt per liter of boiling water.**

108

CRISP SALAD GREENS

The common salad spinner is a must for kitchens that put out a high volume of fresh vegetables and salads. Prep time spent washing and rinsing produce can be tedious.

CHEF SAYS

"Spinning allows you to rinse fast and dry even faster. Without a spinner, lettuce and produce becomes waterlogged from rinsing too long or crushed and wilted from patting dry to aggressively, or worst of all, gritty and sandy from not being properly washed at all."

Thin Slice with a Mandolin

Chef says

Unless you can master the art of consistent, perfectly thin slicing, get a mandolin.

The Chef is not big on kitchen gadgets, but his one saves immense time and delivers the building blocks for many visually impressive plating techniques.

Paper thin cucumber, apple, beet or aubergine can serve as an eye pleasing perimeter to towers and salads and is a must for layered baked dishes.

Thin potatoes are a must for wrapping fish and meat in fancy wellington and croute dishes.

The Mandolin also makes shredding a breeze.

"NOTHING WOULD BE MORE TIRESOME THAN EATING AND DRINKING IF GOD HAD NOT MADE THEM A PLEASURE AS WELL AS A NECESSITY."

~VOLTAIRE

Whipped Cream

Well executed whipped cream elevates any desert.

Prepare

A cold bowl

Put a steel mixing bowl in a freezer for 10 minutes.

Add **2C (480ml)** fridge-cold, heavy (double) cream.

Hand whisk much faster than you think and much lighter than you expect until peaks form.

Add **2T Caster sugar,** halfway through mixing.

Fold in **1t vanilla, cognac or dark rum** once cream is whipped

The Spectrum of 5 flavors

Flavor profiles can be understood by identifying the following:

Sweet, Sour, Salty, Bitter, Spicy

& Pungent (Umami)

Chef says

"Every food culture has local ingredients to fill the 5-flavor spectrum. Experiment with the ingredients of a specific region or culture.

Start with a simple mix of equal parts sweet and sour. From there, experiment by adding components of spice, and pungency, adding "salty" at the end to bring the concoction together.

Use these fundamentals to mix up a dressing, marinade, reduction or braising liquid.

Experiment with Sweet

honey, maple syrup, molasses, brown sugar, palm sugar, reduced apple or pineapple juice

Experiment with Sour

vinegar (cider, red-wine, champagne, balsamic, rice wine)

citrus (lemon, lime, grapefruit, orange)

dry wine, sherry, masala, rice wine

Experiment with spicy, pungent and salty

Chili, red pepper, ginger, garlic, shallot, Asian fish sauce, soy sauce, miso paste,

118

Chimichurri Sauce for Grilled Meat

Popular in the grill-heavy cultures of Argentina and Uruguay, this family of tangy oil and vinegar concoctions has close relatives in many cuisines. It performs minor miracles as a marinade or finishing sauce for meat or as a dressing for warmed vegetables.

Chef says

"The zip, bite and pungency of vivid green Chimichurri acts as a poetic foil to the heady char of steak, hot off the grill"

Prepare

Whisk, stir or shake to combine

1C (240ml) olive oil or other dressing oil

6T red Wine Vinegar

2C (480g) chopped Parsley

4 cloves fine chopped garlic

$1/4$ t red Chili Flakes

$1/2$ t salt (or to taste)

Experiment

by adding the following

$1/2$t smoked Paprika

1t lemon zest

1t ground Cumin

2T chopped fresh oregano

Swap the parsley with mint or cilantro (coriander)

The Omelet

Chef Says

"The humble omelet is often considered a bellwether of a cook's kitchen prowess"

The perfect omelet is fluffy with only the taste of fresh egg. It is never dry, rubbery or tough. Like most eggs, the omelet is cooked exclusively in butter. The real secret here: The Chef throws in a dash of water to create steam, delivering a slightly fluffy texture.

Prepare

Thoroughly stir or whisk **3 whole eggs** and **1T water**.

Heat **1T butter** over medium heat until foam subsides.

Pour in egg mixture

As egg cooks, push in edges and tilt pan to allow any liquid egg to contact pan.

As curd forms, add **2T filling** down the center line.

As curd and edges become dry, fold sides up (into thirds) and roll onto plate.

Season, garnish, and present.

Experiment

Add creamed spinach, mushrooms, marinated artichoke hearts, chives, sun-dried tomato, cheese, chopped ham.

A Family of Oils

The Chef's oil collection looks like a painter's palette and each oil has a specific job.

Experiment with low-heat, sauté Oils

The Chef sautés and pan cooks with oils that have a fairly high smoke-point and subtle flavor.

medium bodied extra virgin olive oil, peanut oil, almond oil, avocado oil, grape seed oil ...and of course, many dishes call for butter or lard.

Experiment with high-temperature Frying Oil

For hot pan searing and seep frying, high smoke point and economy are paramount.

sunflower oil, safflower oil, peanut oil

Experiment with Finishing Oils

Finishing oils come in notoriously small bottles and are exclusively for application after a dish is off the heat, just before serving *(pg. 47)* or for use in dressings *(pg. 41)*. Besides adding bright, unique flavors, they are a fantastic visual appetizer.

walnut oil, hazelnut oil, toasted sesame oil, fruity extra virgin olive oil

The Chef doesn't use generic vegetable oil (commonly soy, corn or rape seed) for much of anything.

DON'T CROWD THE PAN

Whether boiling, sautéing, or deep frying; do it in small batches. A crowded pan reduces cooking temperature and adversely affects cooking results.

Sauté in a single layer. Deep fry and boil a quantity that can float in a single layer. Plan ahead to allow enough time for multiple small batches.

CHEF SAYS

"Only disappointment can ensue when sautéing turns into steaming and deep-frying turns into a soggy oil soaking affair."

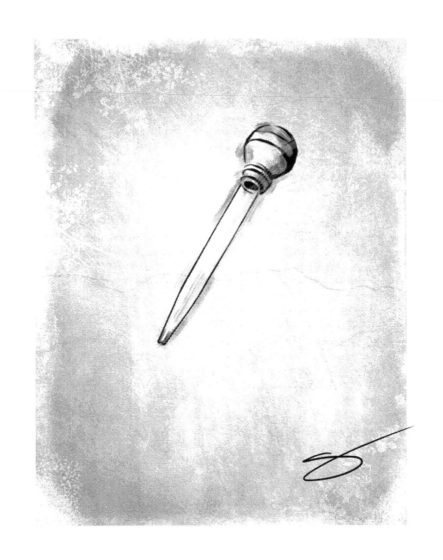

BASTE A ROAST

Anytime there is a big hunk of meat in the oven or sauté pan, The Chef labors, basting it continuously to keep it moist and flavorful.

Cooking meat, fish and poultry renders out the valuable juices and fats. These are the elixirs of flavor. Use a large spoon, ladle or basting pipe to put these drippings back onto and into the dish.

CHEF SAYS

"The difference between appallingly dry and lusciously tender is in the basting. If there are no natural juices, add your own; baste with stock, butter, oil or animal fat"

128

A Fireplace and a River ~ Kilin, Scotland

In Killin, Scotland, the wide river rushes right through the middle of town, forking in two, under a stone bridge that is only wide enough for one car. Here, where the river forks, the water is foaming and rushing over a wide cascade of black rocks. The froth is tinged tan because of the sediment that it captures from the trickles and rivulets that filter through the soggy, rolling peat hills of the Highlands to the north.

When you turn your back to the river, you face across the lane to a set of heavy black doors and the many little square windows of a restaurant. When it's cold enough - which is usually - there is a column of smoke rising steady from the fat, stone chimney up high on the peaked roof.

When you push through a second set of unpainted, brown wooden doors, you are in a small dining room that will always have someone else already eating or at least drinking a glass of whiskey. In the back of the dining room, there is a long bar of heavy, lacquered wood, as thick as your wrist, shining from candles in black iron holders. The wall behind the bar is nothing but bottles of gold and copper single malt Scotch whiskey. Some are in fancy holders, made of metal or wood or red velvet, that cover up the lower half of the bottle.

When you sit down at a table, it is impossible to be far away from the massive carved hearth that takes up the whole side-wall. The hearth extends deep back into the stone, to frame a fire-box where there is an iron rack, hung from chains, that holds a layer of hot coals. The rack used to be the forge for the blacksmith that worked here and so it still has a floor vent to draw up air to keep the coals bright red-hot and smoking; the smoke getting sucked up fast through the chimney. The room is always full of an earthy, peaty smoke smell and the heat from the coals can be felt from across the room.

The best dishes to have for dinner on a blowing, autumn night are the thick soups and the hearty baked dishes. Some nights, you'll get Cullen Skink; a creamy bisque of smoked Finnan haddock. onions and potatoes that has a deep smoky smell and the ocean smell of the docks when the net boats come back in the early morning. The soup stays very hot so you start by dunking in thick cuts of buttered bread. The baked dishes are pies or galettes in the French style; hand rolled pastry shells folded over to hold an oozing mix of aubergine

129

and tomato and a smooth blue-veined goat's cheese. The tang from the goat's cheese makes you want to sip your ale in between each bite. The crust is flaky and sweet and you use it to mop up the last bits of the filling, which is still hot and melted.

There are sweet things for pudding too: Usually crumbling cakes and tarts that are just sweet enough to stand up to whiskey. The cakes have subtle flavors like anise and lavender and one pudding is always enough for two people because they are heavy and satisfying.

The restaurant is open all year, and is much more popular during the warm, short summer when wealthy travelers come from the big cities of Edinburgh and Glasgow to walk the Highlands and climb the Munro peaks, but I mostly remember the feeling of autumn here, because that is when the sky is still clear and crisp, but it is plenty cold to need the big fireplace full of the hot coals heating up the whole room. It is also when the malt whiskey tastes the best and warms you the most.

Killin, Scotland 2011

The Crouton and "Panzanella"

Panzanella is a simple salad based around perfectly crunchy yet slightly chewy cubes of pan fried bread. The dish usually relies on fresh tomatoes, but the Chef throws in whatever fresh veggies are on hand that day.

Prepare the perfect crouton

Cut **1 loaf day old crusty peasant-style bread** into 1" cubes

Heat **2T butter or oil** and add bread cubes tossing until browned and toasted **(10 minutes)**

Prepare the Salad

Toss croutons with

2 whole tomatoes roughly chopped

1 red or yellow bell pepper diced large

1 peeled cucumber cut in 1" cubes

Half of one red onion, thinly sliced

$1/4$ C shredded basil leaves

Liberal salt and pepper to taste

3T vinaigrette *(pg. 41)*

Chef says

"I love the reaction to this bright, flavorful, texture-rich salad when the guest was expecting just another 'lettuce and something' affair."

134

TEMPER YOUR TABLEWARE

Whether hot dish or cold, prepare your serving platters, and table service by warming or cooling appropriately.

The Chef gives his bowls and plates **3-8 minutes** in a warm oven **(140-180°F) (60-80°C)**. Likewise, The Chef places service for cold dishes in the refrigerator for **20 minutes** prior to service.

CHEF SAYS

"The perfect recipe is only perfect at the right temperature. Don't let a cold plate steal glory from your meal. Nothing disappoints like wilted salad, or tepid soup."

136

Aioli in an Instant

French, Spanish and many other Mediterranean cultures pair earthy dishes with this silky, garlic emulsion. Even simple bread becomes a proper first course when accompanied by aioli.

Prepare

In a blender or small food processor (or mortar and pestle if you're feeling rustic) combine until smooth: **2 cloves garlic, 1 room temperature egg.**

While whisking, blending or stirring; drizzle in **1C (240g) neutral oil (grape seed, or light olive oil)** in a steady stream.

Once thickened to mayonnaise consistency, stir in **¹/₄ t salt** and **¹/₂ T fresh lemon juice or vinegar.**

Serve with bread, vegetable, meat and egg dishes.

Experiment by adding

¹/₂ t loose saffron threads steeped in 1t warm water

1t lemon zest

¹/₂ t smoked paprika

¹/₂ t chopped marjoram, thyme or dried red chili

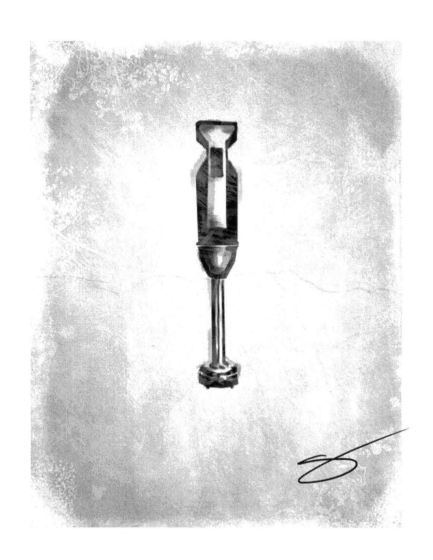

THE IMMERSION BLENDER FOR SOUP

There are numerous ways to pulse good ingredients down
into soup, but the quickest and cleanest is the simple
immersion blender. Quickly turn a cauldron of chunky
stewed ingredients into a rustic or silky-smooth soup.

CHEF SAYS

*"If you must use a food processor or carafe blender, fill it
less than half full and get a good hold of the lid. Hot liquids
expand and are notorious for blowing the lid right off. No-
one is impressed with soup on the ceiling."*

Don't forget to hit your soup with a dollop or drizzle of
something to finish. *(pg. 47, 81)*

Salt for Cooking -Salt for Finishing

Every kitchen should have a variety of salts at the ready. Cooking salt should be easy to handle, flavorful, and be fairly economical.

Finishing salt should be exotic, flavorful and provide a treat for the eyes

Experiment with Cooking Salt

kosher salt, large grain sea salt, natural mineral salt

Experiment with Finishing Salt

Grey salt

Fleur de sel

Hawaiian red salt

Himalayan red mineral salt

Chef says

"Pasta water gets cooking salt, a quenelle of foie gras gets a pinch of finishing salt. No dish gets iodized table salt."

Compound Butter

Compound butter (a fancy term for butter with stuff mixed into it) always impresses. Luckily for the Chef, it is very simple to make

Prepare

Finely chop **2T of herbs** or other fragrants (**chive, thyme, rosemary, tarragon, lemon zest, garlic, black pepper, saffron**) and incorporate into **2T mild oil** *(pg. 23)*.

Warm over medium heat until softened and fragrant.

Chop **2C (480g) butter** into small cubes and mash (by hand or with a stand mixer and whisk attachment) until butter softens and lightens in color

Blend in herb and oil mixture to incorporate thoroughly.

Spoon mixture into a log shape on flat butcher's paper.

Roll into 2-inch diameter tubes.

Chill in refrigerator for **30 minutes.**

Chef says

"Slice off healthy knobs and serve on poached fish, grilled steaks, sautéed vegetables or anything else that you want to elevate to luxury cuisine."

144

Finishing Pasta

One of most neglected techniques when cooking pasta is the final step of marrying the flavors of noodle and sauce.

Prepare

Cook quality dry (or homemade fresh) pasta just shy of "al dente" (**1 to 2 minutes less** than the package instructions)

Drain pasta (no rinsing, no adding oil), reserving a half-cup of the foggy, starchy cooking water

Toss drained pasta into sauté pan with simmering sauce and cook through for **one minute.**

Add starchy pasta water to the mix a tablespoon at a time to loosen sauce if necessary.

Chef says

"Perfect harmony is the perfect pasta to sauce ratio. Think of dressing a salad with vinaigrette: Nobody likes soggy salad or swimming noodles"

146

SAIGON ~ A POP-UP LUNCH

In Saigon, by breakfast time, the heat is already threatening in its heavy, hazy way. Breakfast is when I watch what I consider to be the most amazing parade of culinary industry anywhere on the planet.

As soon as the sunlight comes in through the thin curtain, I make my way from the hotel room, past the morning porter, to the lobby, with its deceptively chilled air. When the doors open to the outside, the sounds and the heat hit you with a crash. Turning right, through the narrow alley, the sounds are of cooking; heavy pots of broth for the day's noodle soups. The locals in Saigon eat the noodle soup for breakfast; a hot broth of beef bones, fish sauce and lemongrass that fills the alley with the scent of citrus and basil. The other noise of Saigon, morning or night, is the droning buzz of mopeds, their horns bleating out constantly, like a fast moving flock of sheep being brought to market.

I usually skip the local's breakfast, walking past them all squatting on the tiny, red, plastic stools, slurping noodles and wiping their mouths with small squares of paper. I usually stop at the café on the Rue Catinat – the only café with full-size wicker chairs – and have a baguette and an oily black Vietnamese style coffee that drips through the metal filter over a layer of sweetened condensed milk.

From the tables on the Rue, against the background blur of the mopeds come the little old ladies wearing their navy blue peasant smocks and their pointy straw hats with the bright scarfs holding the hats down onto their heads. Each lady shuffles slow in woven sandals. Over her shoulder is a long stick and on each end of the stick is a woven basket. The baskets are piled high with fresh ingredients and pots and pans that will become a fully operational restaurant by lunchtime. In one basket there will be an iron stove and an ashy block of charcoal for heating. There will be a cauldron for broth, or a wok for frying. There will be rice noodles and maybe tofu or sticky rice cakes. There will also be bunches of mint, basil, and fragrant coriander. The other basket will have the furniture and the place settings. The furniture is a stack of the small red plastic stools. The place settings are white and blue bowls, chopsticks soup spoons, and small glasses for the cool green tea that will get served. Each lady will set her restaurant up in the same place each day and she'll serve mostly the same local regulars every day.

The best lunch I ever had from one of the stick and basket ladies was up north in Hanoi, on a street corner across from the heavily guarded Mausoleum where the embalmed body of Ho Chi Minh

147

rests under bright orange lights. The lunch was small rectangles of tofu; the kind with a salty outer skin. The tofu was deep fried crispy and placed on a metal rack to cool. With the tofu, you got bunches of sticky rice noodles that had been soaked until soft and cut into squares that were easy to handle. With these, you got a small bowl of dipping sauce; rice vinegar, fish sauce and flecks of bright red chili pepper. You also got a heaping bunch of green and purple basil. You would use chopsticks to gather up a bunch of the basil and wrap it around the tofu or noodles and dunk the whole mouthful into the dipping sauce. I remember on this day that when I sat down, I was one of only a few people being served. By the time I got up, the street corner was full of twenty or more people, having borrowed red plastic stools from other street food vendors nearby.

There are a lot of ways to eat well in Vietnam, but without fail, each morning I wake up and immediately start thinking about which of the little old lunch ladies I am going to visit that day. This is one of the best things to contemplate while you sit and drink your Vietnamese coffee on the Rue Catinat.

Saigon, 2012

Separating Eggs

For speed, ease and cleanliness, The Chef separates yolks from whites by hand.

Crack a single whole egg into a cup.

Lift out yolk by hand - allowing the white to gently slip off and flow through slightly spread fingers - and set aside.

Pour the successfully separated white into larger collecting bowl, one white at a time.

Chef Says

"A little white in the yolk never hurt anyone. A little yolk in the white is a problem, and will keep the whites from ever becoming frothy and light for merengue or soufflé."

"The less contact with the shell, the better. Shell contact can rupture the yoke and transmit bacteria."

"Custard cream, pasta and ganache are good uses for extra yolks. Merengue and soufflés are a good use for extra whites."

Mash Beyond Potatoes

The heartiness and richness and bold color of a good mash is always welcome on a plate.

Chef says

"A creative mash is a great foundation for an impressive ring mold stack." (see pg. 43)

Prepare

Peel and cut **2 lbs. root vegetables** into 1-inch cubes

Boil in salted water until very tender, but not crumbly or waterlogged (about 10 minutes).

Mash with hand masher or food mill adding milk or cream to reach desired consistency. Season and serve with compound butter *(pg. 143)* or gravy *(pg. 75)*

Experiment with Vegetables

Sweet potato, carrot, turnip, parsnip, sun-choke, acorn or butternut squash.

Experiment with Flavors

2T chopped garlic

6 cloves mashed, roasted garlic

2T shopped herbs: Rosemary; thyme; tarragon

4T caramelized, diced onion or shallot

1/4 t nutmeg, cinnamon or allspice

4T crispy bacon or pancetta

MAGIC MERINGUE

One of the most noble deserts; fluffy peaks of glossy merengue are as impressive as they are elusive. Warming the mix is the secret.

In a room temperature mixing bowl, combine:

7 large egg whites *(pg. 151)*

¹/₂ t cream of tartar

Hand whisk fast until glossy and stiff (6-7 minutes). Whisk in ²/₃ **C granulated sugar** (**1T at a time**)

CHEF SAYS

"For creamy merengue as a topping, mix the affair over a Bain Marie: (a saucepan of simmering water) to warm slightly. This results in glossier, taller meringue that holds shape"

For crisp, baked meringue, turn stiff merengue out in mounds onto a baking sheet and into a **300°F (150°C)** oven. Immediately reduce to **275 °F (135°C)** and bake until lightly browned (**about 30 minutes**). Turn off oven and leave baked meringues in the oven until cooled completely (**about 90 minutes**).

Puff Pastry: A Touch of Class

Many posh kitchens have a stack of frozen puff pastry sheets in the freezer for tartlets, galettes, pot-pies and wellingtons.

Any mix of ingredients can be elevated to the top of the menu by finding a way to package them in puff-pastry.

Experiment

Ratatouille, melanzane, moussaka or any other casserole type mixture.

Chef says

"A piping hot, flaky, pastry galette oozing cheese is a guaranteed crowd-pleaser. Nobody suspects that it is the week's leftover vegetables."

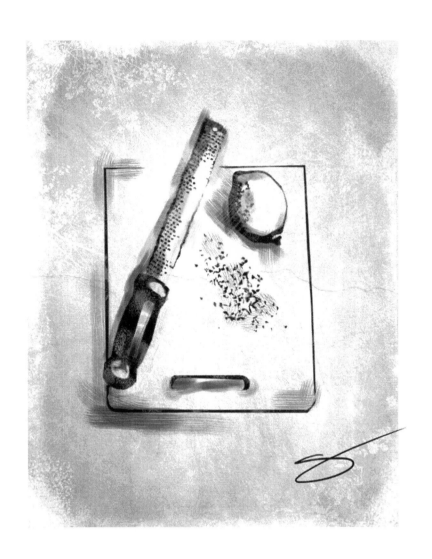

THE RIBBON GRATER

Borrowed from the bench of the woodworker, the ribbon grater makes quick, clean work of grating cheese, zesting citrus and rasping spices.

EXPERIMENT

Grating hard cheese; Pecorino, Parmesan, Roncal, Montsec

Zesting citrus; lemons, limes, oranges

Rasping spices; fresh nutmeg, allspice, clove, star anise

CHEF SAYS

"Whoever first brought this from the carpentry bench into the kitchen is a genius. I don't know how we got by without it."

"But don't neglect the classic barman's zester. Sometimes long, visible curls of zest are just the thing."

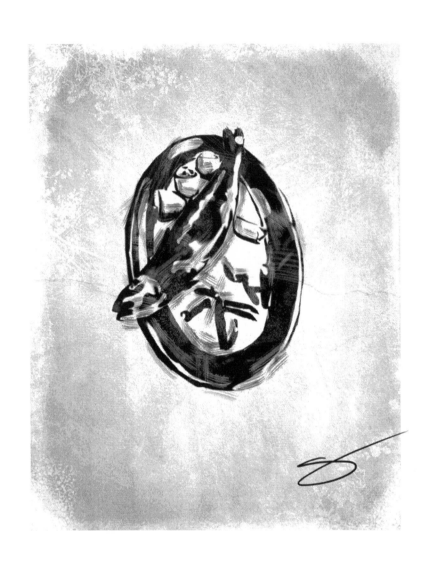

Bring Home the Best

The Chef journeys to the market - or farmers market, deli, butchery, fish-monger, bakery - sincerely believing that he will leave with the single best rendition of the ingredient he is after.

Chef says

"Two-thirds of the success of your meal is already decided once you've left the market.

Ask questions, sample the wares, sniff, squeeze and poke the produce."

Order Something Good

When spending your hard earned time and money to visit a restaurant, consider the strong suits and weak suits of the restaurant kitchen before ordering.

Avoid Pastas, Risottos and other pulses as they are usually par-cooked and flash- finished just before serving, and frankly, you can do a better job at home.

Restaurants are good at elaborate multi-ingredient, time-intensive dishes that thrive when prepared in quantity and benefit from resting, stewing, brining or poaching.

Good Candidates

soups, stews, marinated and stock-based dishes.

braised and slow-cooked dishes (duck confit, coq au vin)

pizza (from a high-heat wood or stone oven)

steaks and chops (from high-heat broilers)

Chef says

"Don't order it if you can do it better at home. If you've made the effort to go to a restaurant, order something that you can't or wouldn't normally make in your own kitchen."

Cooked Meat Must Rest

No Matter what animal it came from, how you got it or how you intend to eat it, grilled, roasted, or broiled meat must be allowed to rest, undisturbed, (ideally, under a foil tent) for **5-10 minutes** (longer for larger pieces) to allow the natural juices to rejoin the body of the meat.

Generally, any juices that began in the meat should stay there. This means that when cooking steaks, chops, burgers, and sausages:

No poking

No pressing

No stabbing.

Prepare

Bring meat to room temperature

Pat the meat dry

Season the meat just before cooking

Cook the meat; sear, grill, roast, braise.

Let the meat rest for 5-10 minutes

Fruit Envy: Cobbler and Crisp

Every season presents an all-star fruit that can be made into a sublime desert. The Chef need only decide on how to embellish it..

Prepare the Fruit

Mix together the filling of

3C (720g) fruit (apple, stone fruit, berries, etc.)

1C (240g) sugar, 1t vanilla, 1 pinch cinnamon, 1 T Lemon Juice (juice of one half lemon), ½ T flour

Pour into a baking dish and cover with

Cobbler crust

Mix 2C (480g) flour, 2t baking powder, 4T sugar, 8T cold butter (cut into pieces), 1C (240ml) cold milk

OR
Crisp / streusel topping

1C (240g) flour, 8T sugar, ½ C oats (or crushed crackers or cookies), 1t cinnamon, 8T butter (cut into pieces)

Let either topping rest for 10 minutes, before spooning over the fruit mixture.

Bake Cobber or Crisp at 375°F (190°C) for 20-30 minutes.

Serve

with cold heavy cream, whipped cream *(pg. 115)*, mascarpone, crème fresh or vanilla ice cream

THE ROAST CHICKEN

Chicken can be roasted a million different ways; most of them dry and bland with soggy skin. For a perfectly crisp and juicy chicken, take a cue from the French and lean heavily on butter, rotate the bird four times, and baste constantly.

Pre-heat oven to 400°F (200°C)

Stuff one well-reared, organic, free-range chicken with **desired herbs**. (The Chef recommends two lemon halves, two whole garlic cloves, 4 sprigs of thyme.)

Truss chicken, or simply tuck wings and legs

Pat dry, season liberally with salt and pepper

Place chicken in a roasting pan with a wing side up. Place **4T of butter** on top.

Roast for **15 minutes**.

Rotate chicken onto its back, baste and roast for **15 minutes**

Rotate chicken onto the opposite wing side, baste and roast for **15 minutes**.

Rotate chicken upright, breast up, baste and roast for **30 minutes** or until juices run clear.

Serve with mash *(pg. 103, 153)* and gravy *(pg. 75)*

CHEF SAYS

"This treatment guarantees a chicken that is juicy and well browned on all sides. The drippings are perfect for gravy or pan roasting vegetables if desired."

Fresh, Local, Seasonal, Organic

(In that order)

Chef says

"Buy your ingredients for flavor, not appearance, size, or luxury. A dish is nothing more than the ingredients. Fuss, technique, exclusivity and complexity cannot make a triumph out of poorly reared, out of season ingredients."

Rome ~ A Meal without a Menu

Just past the weeping trees towering from the stone walls above, we descend gray stairs, damp because they never see the sun. This is hardly the Rome of the Coliseum and the Spanish steps, and yet, it is still Rome; maybe more Rome. Today has been full of a Rome that I have never known: Back alleys and hidden parks, rail lines and hanging laundry. Now, as the sun sets, and the echoes of the small street take over from the roar of traffic, yet another Rome.

The stairs pour out onto a tiny, sloping street, barely wide enough for the miniature cars parked on the one side and the even smaller cars squeezing past. This street is certainly on a map, but who would ever pick it out? We are only here because the stairs end here.

The thinking is that this narrow, unnamed street of worn cobbles will feed onto a larger street that will deliver us among established, attractive dinner options. It may, but we won't find out tonight. Tonight has other plans for us. As the dusk deepens and we walk with echoing footsteps, the only thing to focus on is a man leaning against a wall with a cigarette, a smart checked shirt, and those colored pants only found on the continent. As we pass, we look at him because these things and his impossibly tousled Roman hair can't be ignored. He looks at us because we are the only other thing in the street to look at. He is leaning at the wall, next to a set of open double-doors. It is the open doorway now that can't be ignored and he watches us watch the opening, and he smiles knowingly. In the double doorway opening sits a large lady in a black leather chair with a sleeping or dead dog at her feet. She - the lady – is not moving, is wearing round, black, Breakfast at Tiffany's sunglasses and very red lipstick. She is also smoking. Behind the large lady are three thick, overlapping plates of glass with cracks and what look like bullet holes. The glass must surely be art. To the left of the large lady are tables that are set for dinner. The tables are why we stop and stare.

To our stopping and staring, the leaning guy pinches the cigarette away from his mouth and says flatly "You should eat here. It is very good", then the cigarette is plugged back in to his lips.

To enter, we walk in front of the lady, who remains motionless, like the blind bathroom attendant in those assassin movies. We step over the dog, who slides his tail once across the floor; his version of a wag. There are other people dining who do not look up at us; like walking through someone else's dream. We sit at an open table; round, white-clothed, and sparsely set. All of this has taken a little faith. There is no sign, there is no chalkboard; no hostess, no menu. We sit and we wait and we look around and we wait more. The only reassurance is a wink from the leaning guy, who is now the sitting guy at a table not far from us.

Then comes what must be the waiter, or the cook or the chef or the owner or the manager; a big guy, heavy cheeks, slick black hair, chef's whites and kitchen clogs. He approaches us with warmth, but not a smile. Hands clasped, he simply asks would we like red wine or white wine. We say red, because it seems like it fits the mood and because it seems too ridiculous to ask what is for dinner.

The big man returns with an uncorked, unmarked bottle of wine. He pours it out, inky and red-black. He comes back again and has food - three antipasti dishes - recognizable as the same three dishes on the tables of our neighbors. One dish is mashed roasted sweet potatoes. They are orange with crispy bits where they are toasted from the oven. They are dry and light and spicy with red pepper. They are spot-on as the first flavor of the night. Another dish is large baked beans in a rusty reddish tomato sauce. The beans are rich and earthy like a rustic Italian take on American ranch beans. The third dish is simple bruschetta: clean, springy bread grilled with black stripes on one side, covered in chopped tomato and olive oil. The bright flavors clean up the palate and the bread proves useful for mopping up the remnants of the tomato sauce from the beans.

We glance around at the few other diners. We are trying to work out what will happen next. It's difficult to say. Some are sitting in front of pasta, some have meat. All have multiple empty bottles of the unmarked wine.

The big man - who is so far the only person running the show - clasps his hands again and simply says or maybe asks "Pasta?" Our blank looks convince him to elaborate and with very few words a decision seems to be made.

The pasta arrives; two bowls, both white and creamy and steaming. One is Cacio e Pepe, wide tubes cooked quite al dente mixed into an emulsion of butter, parmesan cheese and cracked black pepper. The rich, clean, signature dish of Rome. The other is Carbonara: the same firm tube shaped noodles mixed with crisp pancetta, shavings of tart parmesan and a smooth sauce thickened with slightly cooked egg.

We trade bites, comment on the firmness of the noodles, drink loads of the inky red wine and generally do our best to finish the dish and accept the strange vibrations. Sitting, chatting, trying to solve the place, we notice the walls adorned with clues as to what is going on

174

here. Behind me is the most illustrative. It is a review from the New York Times from a few years ago. Gianni runs the Trattoria the way he wants. Operating without a license, under the radar of the health department, this is rustic roman dining at its best. The article suggests we sit back, get into the mood of the place and "…expect to end your meal feeling part of the family and likely dancing on the tables after too much Grappa". And so we continue as advised.

The pasta plates are cleared, more wine is poured and we are served white plates anchored with braised chicken thighs in an earthy mushroom reduction. We do our best, but hardly justice as the scale of the cuisine catches up to us. The din of the place starts to crank up as conversations get more exaggerated and passionate and tables, including ours, are cleared of flatware and set with open bottles of house made grappa and tart limoncello. Accompanying the digestifs are four small orbs of dark chocolate just pungent enough to offset the sweet liqueurs. And this is how the meals go here: You sit and you wait and you eat whatever Gianni wants to cook up that night. The only decisions to be made are "will you eat here?" and "red or white wine?" You can trust implicitly that the decisions beyond that – those that have been made for you – are the right ones. When we are finally ready to carry on with our evening, we ask for the check. Gianni looks at us, scrutinizing, sizing us up and purses his lips. Twenty-five Euros each, and he hands us only an empty silver plate.

We are certainly not the first to discover the place and certainly won't be the last to walk past the blind lady and the sleeping dog. But considering the accidental discovery, and the richness of the day that led to it, we take it as a personal triumph, one easy to romanticize as we sit back, melting into a haze of Grappa, feeling the urge to break into song.

Rome, 2011

175